EDUCATION IN THE SOUTH

EDUCATION IN THE SOUTH

BY
EDGAR W. KNIGHT, Ph.D.
PROFESSOR OF EDUCATION IN THE UNIVERSITY
OF NORTH CAROLINA

Chapel Hill, N. C., U. S. A.
THE UNIVERSITY OF NORTH CAROLINA PRESS
LONDON: HUMPHREY MILFORD
Oxford University Press

COPYRIGHT 1924 BY THE MACMILLAN COMPANY

Reprinted through the courtesy of
THE MACMILLAN COMPANY
From
"Twenty-five Years of American Education"

First impression of this reprint 1924
Second impression of this reprint 1929

PREFACE

This is a brief account of public education in the southern states during the last twenty-five years. It first appeared as Chapter XIV in "Twenty-five Years of American Education," a volume prepared by some of the former students of Professor Paul Monroe, as he rounded out a quarter century of distinguished service to Teachers College, Columbia University, and inscribed as a testimonial of their high esteem for him as scholar and teacher. That volume was edited by Professor I. L. Kandel, of Teachers College, and published by The Macmillan Company. To the editor and the publisher the author is indebted for permission to reprint in this form his contribution on education in the South.

EDGAR W. KNIGHT.

CHAPEL HILL, N. C.

EDUCATION IN THE SOUTH

Introduction

The story of public education during the last quarter-century in those states which had formed the Confederacy is a unique and somewhat remarkable record. But an adequate understanding of it or of the present educational status and problems of the South requires a view not only of the actual educational situation twenty-five years ago but also of the social, economic, and political conditions which had prevailed there for two or three decades following the Civil War. A summary of that situation and an account of those conditions become therefore an important part of the story here to be related.

The Continuing Effects of the Civil War — Educational

The chief need of the South twenty-five years ago was a full and working agreement on education. The principle of universal education at public expense had not yet passed into conviction there. It was still in the academic stage, the topic of the educator and theorist. It had not yet become the interest of the citizen. Compared with the United States as a whole, the Southern states were very backward in education. Public schools were deplorably poor and ineffective. The average annual per capita expenditure for public education in 1897 was $2.62 in the country at large, but in the South it was less than ninety cents and in some Southern states it was less than fifty cents. The amount raised per taxpayer was twice as large and the amount raised for each child of school age was three times as great in the country at large as in the Southern states. The amount of taxable wealth back of each child of school age in the South was only one fifth or one sixth as great as that in the North and the West, where the proportion of adult males to the school population was also fifty to one hundred per cent greater than in the Southern states; and the number of children of school age to every hundred persons of the total population was greater in the South than in any part of the United States. The average monthly salary of teachers in the United States was nearly fifty per cent larger than in the South, where it was less than twenty-eight dollars. In Alabama, Tennessee, and Mississippi the average was only twenty-four dollars and in North Carolina it was only twenty-one dollars. Between 1860 and 1900 the average annual salary of teachers in the South had actually decreased. In some parts of the South teachers received no more for their services than was received for the hire of those who worked under conditions of penal servitude.

Courses of study had somewhat expanded, but poorly equipped teachers and the lack of supervision rendered such courses ineffective and chaotic. The schools were imperfectly graded and methods of teaching were wasteful and deadening. School equipment was likewise poor. The grounds were often one half acre or less in size and the average value of rural schoolhouses as late as 1900 was only one hundred dollars. The average value of school property per child of school age was only one fifth that of the United States. One fifth of all the schoolhouses in North Carolina and Virginia were log, a condition fairly typical of all the South. In Tennessee as late as 1907 one seventh of the schoolhouses were log. In Virginia in that year only 168 of more than 7000 schoolhouses had modern provisions for ventilation. The school term in the South in 1897 was only

93 days, while the term for the entire country was 141 days. In North Carolina it was only 60 days. In some places teachers were employed for half the term in winter, and different teachers in the summer taught the same schools the remainder of the term. Teachers were generally untrained, sometimes very indifferent, and often held in low esteem by the public. From one half to four fifths of them held second- and third-grade certificates, usually the lowest then issued. Eighty per cent of nearly 2800 teachers in Florida held such certificates in 1897, and only 317 of them were graduates of normal schools.

Normal schools and other agencies for training teachers were few and standardless. Certification standards were low and often varied among the counties of the same state. The status of the teacher was so ridiculously low that few promising young people could be persuaded to enter the work. Less than 60 per cent of the school population was enrolled in school and less than 40 per cent was in average daily attendance. Only one pupil out of ten of those enrolled reached the fifth and only one in seven the eighth grade. There was not a public high school of standard grade. Textbooks were often nondescript, and their selection was unintelligent and haphazard and generally optional with local authorities. The public, under such conditions, could not view the schools with pride or even complacency.

The unit of practical school administration in the South twenty-five years ago was the small and weak district. There were no creditable and substantial county school organization and supervision. County superintendents were generally colorless and deficient in leadership, employed for part time and poorly paid for that. The positions usually went to briefless young lawyers, broken-down preachers, country editors, too often as a reward for political service. Each local school was left to itself without aid or counsel from county or state. Its trustees were often chiefly interested in keeping the school near their homes and in employing their relatives or friends as teachers. The policy of multiplying schools had been ruinous. State departments of education were less real than nominal, as a rule little more than clerkships or pitiful political appendages. State superintendents were seldom educational statesmen and leaders but politicians, lawyers, soldiers, or patriots. Rarely were they selected for professional fitness, and the conditions of the office generally made them clerks.

No Southern state had any compulsory attendance legislation although thirty-two of the United States had enacted such laws. The subject was often favorably discussed by groups of school workers and resolutions favoring such legislation were adopted. But bills introduced into the legislatures usually met with the specious argument that the school system was not ready for such a step. Lack of sufficient physical equipment for schools often gave such argument respectful hearing, but the force of the industrial revival then gaining in the South undoubtedly was strong. Practical state-wide legislation on the subject did not come for many years. The state superintendent in North Carolina in 1898 recommended "a mild form of compulsory legislation to begin with," but action was delayed. When compulsory attendance legislation was finally enacted in the South, it was usually optional in character and in some of the states required a majority vote of the electors in the county or district to adopt; and when adopted, the law required attendance only for a minimum term and with exemptions so numerous as to render it ineffective.

Child labor laws were slowly enacted in the South, where, with the rise of cotton factories, boys and girls of school age quickly became a part of that pathetic industrial force known as child labor. Industrial reforms were needed as an essential part of necessary educational progress. But a warfare was waged between the system of child labor on the one side and industry, the parent, the child, and even democracy on the other; those who worked for such reforms conceived them and education as two important phases of the movement for a more nearly democratic order. In 1900 nearly thirty per cent of all the operatives in the cotton mills of Alabama were under sixteen, and in the entire South one fourth of them were under that age. Eighteen per cent of the textile operatives in North Carolina and probably 30,000 in the entire South were under fourteen years of age. The number of children under twelve in factories was probably 20,000. As late as 1900, fully sixty per cent of the operatives in the spinning departments of cotton factories in the Piedmont region were less than sixteen years of age.

These facts reflect not only an unwholesome educational situation in the South twenty-five years ago, but a stubborn and unyielding obstacle to the later development of education there. The chief burden of the painful industrial readjustment of a population then moving from the conditions of agriculture to those of manufacture were too often laid on the child, by argument that legislation restricting the labor of the child was paternalistic and invasive of parental function. Under these conditions, then, why should the South provide money to build schools for the children while the influence of growing industry continued to shut so many of them up in factories? Moreover, thousands of humble families, accustomed to agricultural failures and a vicious crop lien despotism, seemed to see in the new factory instant escape from rural isolation, barrenness, and poverty. What they failed to see, however, was that redemption from these evils by this means would often drive them to others they knew not of, to pitiless helplessness of fixed dependency. Urbanized industrial tenancy was to become and to remain almost as troublesome to the development of schools as farm tenancy has been. Few, even of more exceptional virility, without the aid of adequate child labor and compulsory attendance legislation, could hope to rise out of the enfolding powers of such a system which has consciously served to hold its humble and timid agricultural and industrial forces in a state of arrested development.

Illiteracy was widespread not only among the negroes but among the native whites in the South. Of the native white population ten years of age and over more than twelve per cent were unable to read and write, while in some of the Southern states, especially North Carolina, Louisiana, and Alabama, the percentage was approximately sixteen per cent — one native white person in every six above the age of ten being unable to read and write. The average rate of illiteracy among the native white population for all the other states of the Union was less than three per cent. The menace of illiteracy among the native white population in the South had decreased from 22.7 per cent in 1880 to 12.2 per cent in 1900. But the extent of illiteracy continued a disgrace. Notes of denial and resentment were often heard, but they became less and less occasional as the knowledge of the real significance of illiteracy increased. But the menace could not be removed until frankly faced by the people of the South, until indifference to it rather than illiteracy itself came to be recognized as the greater reproach to that region.

Education in the South had failed to develop and advance as its friends had hoped during the quarter-century following the close of reconstruction. Except in the towns and cities which were stimulated to action by aid from the Peabody Fund, public schools were in bad plight, and even there progress was slow. Public education had not yet been accepted in the South. It was still poverty stricken, bore the odium of bad rule and partisan politics, and was otherwise in disrepute. In consequence, indifference to it was so deadly as to equal outright hostility.

Economic Effects

One of the most immediate causes of these conditions was economic desolation. The Southern states had come out of war with a loss of the greater part of their white adult males and an almost complete loss of their accumulated capital. Factories, public buildings, railroads, houses, barns, farm implements, and seeds had been destroyed. Banks had been ruined. The entire labor system had been demolished, and the negroes, unable quickly to adjust themselves to their new economic status, had preferred restless roving to helping to rebuild the waste places of the South. Public finances were in a perilous condition, with state treasuries depleted and credit abroad lost. Reconstruction had followed and robbed the South of what war had spared. Federal officers were often dishonest, cases of fraud and extravagance were numerous and flagrant, corrupt and ignorant officials and legislatures not only looted treasuries and public funds but imposed enormous taxes and ran their fingers deep into the pockets of posterity by piling up bonded debts totaling more than $300,000,000. Everywhere there was widespread economic depression. Tariff laws oppressive to the South but favorable to the East and pension laws which took many millions from the South to the North combined with other influences to make recovery slow.

The wealth of the South thus lost had been considerable. In 1860 with nearly one third of the population of the United States and less than one fourth of the white population, the South had produced more than one half of the agricultural wealth of the entire country, and this in spite of the handicaps of the many economic disadvantages of slave labor. Moreover, the ante-bellum Southern states had greater industrial ambition and success than has generally been assumed. In 1860 they had an investment of more than $175,000,000 in nearly 25,000 factories of one kind and another. Between 1850 and 1860 they had increased their railroad mileage from 2335 to 10,713, a quadruple gain, exceeding by 400 miles the combined railroad mileage of the New England and Middle States, where a gain of only 91 per cent had appeared in that industry during that decade. This development of railroads in the South represented an investment of more than $220,000,000, which had come principally from southern sources.

In 1860 the South had nearly five and a half billions of the slightly more than twelve billions of the total assessed property valuation of the entire country. The wealth of the South (including the wealth represented in the slaves) had exceeded by $750,000,000 that of New England and the Middle States. But ten years later the wealth of the latter group of states exceeded that of the South by nearly eleven billion. The taxable wealth of the entire South in that year was less than that of New York and Pennsylvania. In 1860 South Carolina had ranked third in wealth in the United States but thirtieth in 1870. Georgia had gone from seventh to thirty-ninth place during that decade, Mississippi from fourth to thirty-fourth, and Alabama from eleventh to forty-fourth. Meantime, values were greatly increasing in other sections of the country. As illustration, South Carolina in 1860 had an assessed property valuation greater by $68,000,000 than the total valuation of Rhode Island and New Jersey, but in 1870 those two states had wealth valued at $685,000,000 more than that of South Carolina. These figures reveal the economic losses in the Southern states. The outcome of four years of war and a decade of reconstruction was complete economic collapse, a catastrophe from which the South has been able only in recent years even partially to recover.

The first problem, therefore, had been to restore the agricultural life of the South — a region of poor roads, poor schools, millions of acres of unused lands, multitudes of mortgages, and no money to finance economic recuperation. The principal resource must be cotton, the demands for which made it the best money crop. During most of these years the South knew nothing but cotton, and the force of agricultural tradition and custom was powerful. Diversity as the remedy for adversity was yet unknown. Efforts to resume economic life consisted in an endless chain of borrowing living expenses while the cotton crop was being made. Lack of crop diversification, lack of working capital, and the system of share farming, cropping, and crop liens, which developed as a result, formed a vicious cycle of economic despotism.

Southern banks borrowed credit from remote sources, usually the North, on the assurance that it would be used only to produce cotton. The coming crop was security. The local merchant borrowed from the Southern banks and in turn gave credit to the local farmer on the same stipulation and promise to raise cotton. The crops were thus mortgaged, often before they were planted, and their value was usually spent before they were harvested. Under the crop lien system the raising of foodstuffs was not encouraged, and prices paid for provisions under this system ranged from 75 to 100 per cent higher than the cash prices. When the cotton was picked, the farmer was forced to sell it, no matter what the price, to the merchant who had "run" or "grub staked" him during the year. The merchant repaid the Southern banks, which in turn repaid the Northern banks, with high interest collected at every point. When this cycle was completed, it was necessary to start it all over again. Slavery did not disappear in the Southern states, therefore, with the emancipation of the negroes. This peculating scheme of crop liens kept them in economic bondage for many years.

Racial Conflict

The racial conflict was another obstacle to schools during the last quarter of the last century. Viewed from the purpose, the process, or the result of reconstruction, the negro had been the center of interest. The issue of mixed schools during that régime had been disastrous to education in the South. The negro's ignorance later played into the hands of the politicians, served to lower political morals, and in time to produce political stagnation, and to make him a barrier to educational advancement generally. The thoughtful white leaders of the South were friendly to him then and have remained his best friends. They considered him educable for work, for improvement, and for useful citizenship. They knew that the right kind of education was the only safe remedy for his condition. And their expenditure of 109 millions out of all too meager school funds for his education between 1870 and 1900 is one of the creditable commentaries on the sober educational opinion of that section. Nevertheless, his exploitation by demagogues and designing politicians during most of that time made him an influence of mischief. Before progress in education could come this had to be removed.

Other Obstacles to Progress

Other obstacles to education which were inherited from the war and reconstruction were defective educational legislation and unsound school organization. Conflicts between the constitutional provisions for schools and legislation enacted under them were often troublesome. Sources of school support were decreased or often entirely cut off by constitutional restrictions. Moreover, the blight of partisan politics was deadening. Few features of public school work escaped its ill effects. Unscrupulous men in offices and local political bosses had learned during reconstruction how to exploit the schools for partisan purposes. Schools came to be regarded as the spoils of political victory instead of opportunities for promoting public well-being, and in many places in the South they have not yet been fully emancipated from this influence.

These are some of the reasons for the low condition of public education in the South twenty-five years ago. It had had its rebirth in poverty and destitution. During its early years it had been nurtured and cherished by a few friends and by fewer zealous but often visionary philanthropists. Often it had been the victim of a very feeble leadership. Occasionally it had been betrayed by petty politicians who were moved less often by principle than the desire to gain partisan advantage. Frequently it was subordinated to pernicious and deadening sectarian dogma. These and other handicaps of inheritance and environment forced public education in the South into a life-and-death struggle until near 1900. Before it could overcome these obstacles and approach a promising maturity and position of increasing respectability new foundations had to be built.

The incentives and basis for educational reform depended first on a substantial increase in economic wealth. The relapses of war and reconstruction had to be outgrown, the orderly processes of production and of exchange had to be resumed, the South had to recover her economic stability. This was to be gained slowly. After 1880 the dominance of agriculture, especially of cotton raising, began to yield place to manufacturing. In that year the value of manufactured products was less by $200,000,000 than that of agricultural products, but by 1900 the products of manufacturing and of mining interests exceeded those of agriculture by nearly $300,000,000. And between 1880 and 1900 the products of Southern factories increased by more than 220 per cent. Capital invested in cotton mills alone increased during that period from $22,000,000 to $113,000,000.

The resources and the deposits of national banks increased nearly 400 per cent each, and their capital was more than doubled during these two decades. Railroad mileage increased 112 per cent, and the true value of all property nearly doubled. During the decade from 1890 to 1900 the total taxable wealth of the South increased nearly fifty per cent. This vast industrial change from field to factory meant the presence of a great social change. Industry was coming more and more to be a force in Southern life. Material wealth was rapidly increasing and formed for the first time since 1860 a substantial basis for an increase in school revenues.

The Reconstruction Period

The race issue which had checked the cause of schools for many years was finally to serve as a powerful influence for educational progress. The single purpose of reconstruction had been to give the ballot to the negro; and the operation of the reconstruction acts of Congress, which formed new governments and created a new political people in the South, was incidental to this one object. Passionate political feelings had been involved at every step of the process. In 1867 Congress had forced negro suffrage on the South when only six of the Northern states permitted it. This sudden and indiscriminate gift of the voting privilege to men entirely unprepared for its intelligent use had produced a régime of riot and rascality during which schools and other means of progress had fallen victim to the vengeance and cupidity of adventurers and malefactors.

But before the last state had been restored to the Union the process of undoing reconstruction was under way. Conflicts over the elimination of the negro from politics were fierce and demoralizing. Open bribery, intimidation, stuffing ballot boxes, the manipulation or falsification of election returns, and the use of tissue ballots had developed into high arts. In one election in South Carolina the number of votes cast was nearly twice the number of the names on the poll books. The imposition of the poll tax and the creation of "shoestring" election districts to include sections of dense negro population served to eliminate negro votes or to render them ineffective. By these and other devious ways the dangers of negro domination were somewhat averted during a decade or more following the close of reconstruction. Moreover, a new political movement in some parts of the South threatened division among the Democrats and encouraged the factions in skillful attempts to control the negro vote which had always been purchasable and which was now powerful and dangerous because it was uncertain. The wits of the factions bidding for the negro vote were pitted against each other. In one election, in order to insure their votes, the poll taxes of the negroes were paid by one political faction. The other faction placarded all public places with the extraordinary announcement that poll tax receipts would be accepted for admission to the circus which was to give its performance on election day, and the negroes preferred the show to the polls. But such elimination methods as these were unpleasant. New and less crude devices wearing at least the color of legality had to be found for eliminating the negro from politics. Open and avowed suppression of the negro vote appeared safer and more respectable than fraud and chicanery, even though the legal devices found for contravening the purpose of the Fifteenth Amendment were not lacking in artful subterfuge.

Mississippi led off in 1890 and was shortly followed by other states. The payment of all taxes legally demanded for the two preceding years was set up as one prerequisite for the privilege of voting. Another was the ability of the voter to read and properly to interpret, under the close scrutiny of white election officials, any section of the Constitution. These requirements eliminated large numbers of negro votes and greatly reduced the chance of negro voters to qualify. Finally, the famous "grandfather clause" practically guaranteed the supremacy of the white vote by giving the privilege of voting to those citizens or the descendants of those citizens who had the privilege prior to January 1, 1867, without regard to property or educational qualifications. The vote of the negro thus quickly dwindled into negligible proportions and his political equality became more nearly extinct in law than it had long been in fact. The final stage of the unfortunate reconstruction controversy closed, therefore, in a complete reversal of the purpose and process which marked its beginning. Meantime, however, the schools had been subordinated and often sacrificed to less worthy interests and the education of both whites and blacks had fallen pitiably into neglect. Public energies which should have been spent for schools and for rebuilding Southern civilization were necessarily used to wrest the government and political power from the blacks and their allies. And in some Southern states educational conditions were less wholesome at the close of the century than they had been in 1860.

The Beginnings of Educational Progress

Thus the race issue which for more than two decades after the war had been a very large factor in retarding education became after 1890 one of the strongest influences in promoting it. When the states set up the constitutional requirement of literacy as a qualification for the privilege of voting, to apply ultimately to both races, even for the avowed purpose of eliminating or restricting negro suffrage, they were automatically committed to the enlargement of public educational opportunity. A premium was thus placed on education, and attention was sharply drawn to the imperative necessity for enlarged educational facilities. In the same constitutions which disfranchised the negro or in legislation enacted under such constitutions, requirements were soon made for improving the schools. In Mississippi special taxes were required to increase the school term to four months; in South Carolina the state tax for education was increased so as to provide an annual school revenue of as much as three dollars per child enrolled; in Louisiana provision was made for restoring to the school fund the interest on the lands squandered during reconstruction, and the right of local taxation equal to the state tax for schools was also given the people. Provision was made in Alabama for an increased state school tax, and local taxation for schools was authorized in North Carolina and Virginia.

Restless discontent among the people of the strictly rural sections of the South and radical political changes which marked the closing decade of the last century were other influences which were to hasten the spirit of educational reform. The class consciousness of the farmers had been awakened and had expressed itself through several organizations which were consolidated as the Farmers' Alliance and Industrial Union in 1889. The principal cause of the movement was economic: it sought to win for the farmers conditions under which they might enjoy a just share of their own creations. But it was also concerned with social and political reform. The necessity of the education of the masses was insisted upon by the Alliance which, in resolutions on the subject, held that the uneducated were "always at the mercy of the better informed" and the members were urged to use their influence to secure better educational facilities for their children.

This unrest of the farmer was extraordinary. He had always been accounted so instinctively cautious and conservative that the practical politician had not looked for much shifting in the political allegiance of rural voters. Their isolation had made it difficult to move them suddenly by any impulse sufficient to break party lines and to cause a cleavage from traditional party connections. Dissatisfaction with conditions and with existing leadership, however, produced radical political changes and led to the formation of several political parties. Some of these were the Union Labor Party in Arkansas, the Young Men's Democracy in Louisiana, and the People's Party, also known as the Third Party and the Populist Party. The last named, the strongest of them all, developed organized strength throughout the South and in some cases broke up political associations of a generation and upset the calculations of the most astute politicians. The educational influence of this movement of revolt and of liberation was very evident in Alabama and North Carolina in the nineties, and in all the Southern states it soon became the fashion for all parties to pledge themselves to public school support. By 1900 they were coloring their political platforms with strong declarations of devotion to the cause of public education.

Another foundation for educational upbuilding appeared in a new type of leadership, developed largely through the union of the so-called middle and aristocratic classes. The former through an increase in economic wealth had become more thrifty and influential, and stimulated through the challenge of an awakening democracy they became ambitious for and able to secure some part in public affairs. In antebellum civilization the nonslaveholding whites had not had large place in the essential councils of the South; they had not filled many important offices nor were they allied with the landed and slaveholding classes who had monopolized political power — a monopoly which represented also the supremacy in social and administrative ability.

But the conditions of the new order after Appomattox and reconstruction, by which both the aristocrats and the common people and their property had been depleted, fused both classes more effectively than the South had ever known. The menace of negro power, common suffering, and the bearing of a common burden served to unite them; and in the distribution of political responsibility the South was soon to know no distinction of classes. It was to be democratized in part at least by this fusion of the white people. The South was, happily, to maintain those old dignities and reverences which power and social usage always develop; but to these was to be added another deep force — a quickened sense of responsibility and of liberality toward those who had been unprivileged. By these means aristocracy was to pass and the plain people were to begin to share in the privileges of government. There was to be an upward movement among the masses, now drawn more closely together and led to seek through ambition and industry and the unity of their civic heritage the means of opportunity for all.

The restoration and the preservation of the best in Southern life became a passion with this new leadership as it became conscious of opportunity and power. It viewed with impatience the educational weaknesses of the time and insisted that the truth about the schools be told. It attacked demagoguery and attempts to exploit the public mind with vain boasts of exaggerated achievements. It secured response to the needs of the people through interest in an extension of public school opportunities, which always becomes necessary and inevitable as democracy becomes a reality. The program of this new leadership was the rehabilitation of the South, and in it the desire to enlarge educational opportunity became a form of civic and patriotic piety, even a common faith. The chance for democracy was thus made brighter as the unprivileged and the poor and the privileged and the rich joined hands to build a common school system for all the children.

Thus was prepared the way for educational advance in the South. There had come an increase in wealth. The race issue in politics had been eliminated. The rural people had been awakened, and a new type of leadership had appeared. Many of the stubborn and mischievous difficulties, which for years had stood as a deadly upas to enfeeble social growth, were now in large part removed, and by effort no less heroic and courage no less indomitable than that exhibited during the war. The South now felt a new challenge, a new sense of duty, made more ringing and clear by the conditions of the new order. This sense of responsibility had been personified in Robert E. Lee; it was felt deeply and voiced loudly by leaders of later years, and hereafter it was to lie close to the heart of the New South. And fidelity to it was to bring after Appomattox victories more decisive for Southern well-being than any that preceded it.

Educational Propaganda

By the beginning of the present century conditions were ripe and the way prepared for marked advance. Only the organized agencies of propaganda were now needed and these were to appear in large part in the work of the Conference for Education in the South and in the movement represented by the Southern Education Board and the General

Education Board. The first of the organizations, also known as the Southern Conference Movement, the Southern Educational Movement, and the Ogden Movement, grew out of a small conference held at Capon Springs, West Virginia, in the summer of 1898 and known as the Conference for Christian Education in the South. Rev. T. U. Dudley, Bishop of Kentucky, an alumnus of the University of Virginia, late Chancellor of the University of the South, Sewanee, Tennessee, was elected president. At the second conference, held the following year at the same place, the name was changed to the Conference for Education in the South and Dr. J. L. M. Curry, general agent of the Peabody and the Slater Boards, was elected president. The third conference also met at Capon Springs and Mr. Robert C. Ogden, of New York, one of the most sympathetic friends public education in the South ever had, was elected to the presidency and served in that position for many years. To his generous enterprise, resourcefulness, and administrative wisdom much of the success of the conference was due. For several years he invited numerous people in the North who were interested in education to attend these annual meetings as his guests and for their accommodation provided special trains. In this way influential people of the North became acquainted with those of congenial spirit in the South and thus gained a safer knowledge of the perplexing problems and needs of Southern life.

Formal resolutions of the early conferences were significant. They dealt with the importance of thoroughness of elementary instruction, longer school terms, better qualified teachers, and better buildings and equipment, traveling libraries, and industrial education. Impressive also is this resolution of the second conference:

Resolved, That the education of the white race in the South is the pressing and imperative need, and the noble achievements of the Southern

Commonwealths in the creation of common school systems for both races deserve not merely the sympathetic recognition of the country and of the world at large but also give the old and high-spirited colleges and universities of the South a strong claim upon a generous share of that stream of private wealth in the United States that is enriching and vitalizing the higher education of the North and West.

It is of importance to remember in this connection that private, denominational, and state higher educational institutions in the South were then very poor. Most of them were forced to struggle for existence. Between 1898 and 1903 benefactions to institutions of higher learning in the United States had amounted to more than $61,000,000, but little of this money had reached the South. All the Southern colleges combined had at the latter date only 15 millions of the $157,000,000 of productive funds held by the colleges of the United States. Out of eight and a half millions of volumes in college libraries in the United States only one and a quarter million were found in the South. The colleges of the South had only about $1,000,000 invested in scientific apparatus against a total valuation of $17,000,000 for the entire country in 1903. The physical equipment of the colleges of the United States at that time was worth nearly $150,000,000, but less than $9,000,000 of it was found in the South. The total annual income available for higher education in Alabama, Georgia, Kentucky, Louisiana, Mississippi, the Carolinas, and Virginia was $19,000 less than the annual income of Harvard.

Succeeding meetings of the Conference for Education in the South were held in Winston-Salem, Athens, Richmond, Birmingham, Columbia, Lexington, Pinehurst, Memphis, and other cities in the South. At the instance of the conference, the Southern Education Board was organized in 1901 to aid in the development and the wise direction of educational sentiment, and to help secure larger policies for education, by appealing to the resources of taxation and local forces for self-development. The Board neither held nor distributed funds. Extensive and systematic field work was planned with Dr. J. L. M. Curry as supervising director and President Edwin A. Alderman, then of Tulane University, President Charles D. McIver, of the North Carolina Normal and Industrial College, and President H. B. Frissell, of Hampton Institute, as district directors. President C. W. Dabney, then of the University of Tennessee, was selected as chief of the bureau of investigation, information, and publication; and the services of Dr. P. P. Claxton, then of the University of Tennessee, and Professor J. D. Eggleston, Jr., of Virginia, were secured for the bureau of publicity which was established at Knoxville.

The plans and purposes of this novel campaign for education met with the instant approval of the press of the South and the practical support of the leading people at that time engaged in school work in that section. Able advocates of better schools came forward and enlisted their services in the movement: college and university presidents and professors, lawyers, business men, officeholders, and other builders of public opinion. The most practical school questions were discussed in the meetings which were now held throughout the South — better buildings, increased school funds, improved teaching, improved legislation for schools, and more effective educational organization and administration generally. People gathered in schoolhouses, churches, courthouses, public halls, in city and country alike, to hear discussions of the ways and means of improving education for their communities. Popular education was the theme before multitudes, and enthusiasm for it spread widely and grew intimate with the people. Meantime, the General Education Board was formed (1903) for the purpose of wise and systematic coöperation with the

Southern Education Board, to investigate, collect, and present actual facts concerning educational conditions in the South, and to render financial assistance within the discretion of its trustees and the limits of its resources. Its services to education in the South have been large and varied and have formed a wise and effective demonstration of method.

The work of the General Education Board in the South has been in four main directions. Through the United States Department of Agriculture it has made large contributions for the promotion of practical farming, under an agreement begun in 1906. Demonstration farms are employed under supervision of demonstration agents whose work has been far-reaching. State demonstration agents also conduct work among boys and girls under actual farming conditions through boys' and girls' clubs. The promotion of secondary education constitutes another important service of the board which appropriates to the state universities or the state departments of education sums sufficient to pay the salaries and traveling expenses of high school experts. Through this means hundreds of secondary schools have been built and maintained in recent years. In addition to these services the board has made gifts for higher education in the South, as well as in other sections of the country, to increase endowments and equipment. It has also contributed largely to the support of negro schools, mainly those for the training of teachers, and has contributed towards the expenses of two rural school supervisors who work under the direction of state departments of education in each of the Southern states, for the promotion of better educational, economic, and social conditions of the colored people. Other services of the board have been rendered to medical education, schools of education, and the financing of studies or surveys of state school systems.

The Educational Advance

The work of these agencies had a powerful and practical influence immediately on educational development in the South. Active campaigns for better schools and for improved educational facilities generally were promoted, beginning in North Carolina in 1902, in Virginia in 1903, in Georgia and Tennessee in 1904, in South Carolina, Alabama, and Mississippi in 1905, in Arkansas, Florida, and other states in 1908. Most of these campaigns were continued for several years with fruitful results. Improvements appeared in many ways: the educational provisions of the constitutions and laws were revised and strengthened; in a decade school revenues were increased by 100 to 200 per cent; the improvement of schoolhouses was marked; by 1910, the annual school term was lengthened to 121 days; and the enrollment and average attendance increased. Illiteracy decreased, local taxes for schools multiplied, teachers' salaries increased considerably in comparison with those paid in 1900, progress was made in the training of teachers through state-supported normal schools and teacher-training agencies in institutions of higher learning, and the certification of teachers was put on a better basis. The revival movement also gave impetus to the development of high schools, which began to be established in rural communities as an integral part of the state school systems. Interest in the consolidation of the smaller into larger and better graded and better equipped schools began to grow; rural libraries increased; school-improvement and parent-teacher associations were formed; child labor and compulsory attendance legislation expanded; and supervision through a better type of county superintendent began to show improvement.

By 1915 the average annual school term had lengthened

to 130 days. The average term for the United States in that year, however, was approximately 160 days. The average annual salary of all teachers was $328 in the South and $543 for the country at large. The average annual expenditure per child of school age was $8.50 for the South and $22.19 for the United States, and the value of school property per capita of school population was $18 and $79, respectively. Approximately 72 per cent of the school population in the South was enrolled, as against 74 per cent in the United States; nearly 69 per cent of the enrollment (50 per cent of the school population) was in average attendance in the South as compared with 76 per cent of the enrollment (56 per cent of the school population) in the country as a whole. Out of 8906 public high schools reporting a four years' course of study in the United States in 1915, with an enrollment of 1,362,514 pupils (about five per cent of the school population), only 1466 such schools with 150,607 pupils (about two per cent of the school population) were in the South. A recent study of the United States Bureau of Education (*Bulletin*, 1922, No. 11) reports in the Southern states 1575 secondary schools, public and private, approved by the state departments of education and accredited by the state universities. Eight counties in Arkansas, twelve in Florida, sixty-four in Georgia, one in Mississippi, two in Tennessee, four in Louisiana, and two in Virginia are more recently reported as having no public high school of standard grade.

Most of the Southern states still rank low among their sister states. Measured by attendance in elementary and in high school, in length of term, and in expenditure (per child of school age, per child attending, and per teacher for salaries) they ranked among the forty-eight states in 1918 as follows: Texas, 36th; Florida, 37th; Virginia, 39th; Tennessee, 40th; Louisiana, 42d; Georgia, 43d; North

Carolina, 44th; Alabama, 45th; Arkansas, 46th; Mississippi, 47th; and South Carolina, 48th. In that year the waste as a result of nonattendance, due largely to lack of adequate child labor and compulsory attendance laws, was about 33 per cent, with 25 per cent as the corresponding figure for the United States. The percentage of the school population enrolled in high schools of all grades was 9.3 in the United States and 5.1 per cent in the South. The increase in teachers' salaries generally has been substantial, but the average annual salary now paid public elementary and secondary teachers in the South is less than four fifths of the average for the United States.

The explanation of this low educational position is not hard to find. With limited funds the Southern states must provide two systems of education for large numbers of children scattered over wide areas. They have relatively a larger school population than the other sections of the country. For each thousand adult males in these states there are 1279 children of school age, while the corresponding average in the North is 789 and in the West about 600 children. Moreover, the estimated average true value of all property for each child of school age in the South is approximately one third that of the Northern states and one fourth that of the Western states. In addition, there is the disadvantage of sparsity of population in the South. North Carolina, Tennessee, and Virginia are the only Southern states having more than ten white children, and none has an average of ten colored children, of school age to the square mile. Moreover, the policy of separate schools is accepted as permanent. In the Northern states the average density of school population is from three to ten times greater than that of the South, and in the Western states, where the school population is small, it is largely concentrated in the irrigated regions, rich river valleys, and mining towns and is not so widely distributed as in the South.

No fair account of recent educational progress in the South can be given, therefore, without taking these difficulties into account. Those states are rapidly finding their duty, however, not in the measure of their resources for school support but rather in the measure of their needs for it. With less than normal power they have had to bear abnormal burdens. Between 1900 and 1915 the increase in public school expenditures for the United States was 180 per cent, but in the South it was 280 per cent; and the policy of increased expenditures for the enlargement of educational facilities is rapidly coming to be accepted as permanent. The estimated public school maintenance expenditures for the present school year (1922–23) for the states reporting are: Arkansas, nine millions; Florida, ten millions; South Carolina, eleven millions; Georgia, fifteen millions; North Carolina, twenty millions; Louisiana, twenty millions; and Virginia, twenty-two millions. Virginia to-day has public school property valued at nearly thirty-three millions, an increase of nearly 400 per cent since 1910; and the value of schoolhouses erected in North Carolina during the present school year is twenty-five millions, nearly twice the total value of all school property in that state in 1918. The public schools of Alabama between 1918 and 1921 made 74 per cent as much progress as in the period from 1890 to 1918, as measured by the Ayres index numbers for state school systems.

The tendency to improve administrative organization of public education has not, however, made the same progress in the South as in the country at large. Of the nine states in the Union still retaining ex officio state boards of education, four are Southern states — Texas, Florida, Mississippi, and North Carolina — and all the Southern states except Tennessee still elect their state superintendents of schools by popular vote. In seven of these states, county boards are elected by popular vote; but Texas, Florida, Mississippi, South Carolina, and Georgia continue to elect county superintendents of schools by that method. These latter officers are appointed by the county boards of education in North Carolina, Arkansas, Louisiana, and Alabama; by the county courts in Tennessee; and by the state board of education in Virginia. In theory the county, but in practice the district, with many of its traditional functions, is the unit of local school administration. There is a hopeful tendency, however, toward making the county the unit for the support and direction of public schools. Of significance also is the intelligent manner in which several Southern states have recently approached these administrative problems through commissions to study and report on educational conditions.

With the enactment of a compulsory attendance law in Mississippi in 1918 the last of the Southern states became committed to the policy of requiring children between certain ages to attend school for all or some part of the school term. This movement had begun in the South in 1905 with the passage of initial legislation on the subject in Tennessee. North Carolina followed in 1907, Virginia in 1908, Arkansas in 1909, Louisiana in 1910, South Carolina, Texas, Florida, and Alabama in 1915, Georgia in 1916, and Mississippi in 1918. Revisions, extensions, and improvements have been made in some of these states since the introductory enactments, though such legislation is still local and optional in character and very defective, lacking the full force of public approval needed for its complete success.

Child labor legislation, theoretically closely related to compulsory attendance laws, is found in all the Southern states. But reform is needed here also. Some of the states have made beginnings in legislation and practices designed to protect dependent and delinquent children. Perhaps one of the most advanced and complete plans not only in the South but in the country at large is that set up in North Carolina in 1919, providing for county boards of public welfare and a juvenile court in every county with jurisdiction over all delinquent, neglected, and dependent children under sixteen years of age. Improvement has appeared also in general health regulations and the physical examinations of school children and in renewed efforts, largely as a result of the war, to eliminate illiteracy, with which the South is still shamefully burdened.

Other hopeful signs of educational progress appear in the tendency to improve the status of the public school teacher by raising and standardizing the qualifications to teach and by making provision for the teachers to meet the requirements by enlarging teacher-training facilities. The tendency is toward state rather than county certification and toward accrediting approved university and college diplomas and accepting credentials of teachers from other states.

The Task for the Future

To furnish the kind and amount of education now needed in the South further reform and reorganization seem necessary. More emphasis must be placed on expert educational leadership and direction throughout. The traditional ex officio state boards of education need to be replaced by boards of representative men and women who are recognized for their sane and progressive attitudes toward, and demonstrated ability to promote, public school work. The demand likewise is for a change in the selection of the state superintendent. He is potentially the most strategic officer of the average American state, and the duties of his office require a high order of business and executive ability and professional skill which can never be guaranteed by popular election and which are rarely ever at home with those characteristics which usually commend men to political leaders and party bosses. The choice of a state superintendent of schools should not be limited to the narrow bounds of the state, which is necessary when selection is by popular election. There is needed also a more enlightened county board of educational control, chosen from the citizens at large, for reasonably long terms, and with powers and duties similar to those of city school boards, and selected for recognized ability to direct the large enterprise of public schools in the county rather than for political reasons. A new conception of the office of county superintendent is also urgently needed in the South. Popular elections have no proper place in filling such an office, the duties of which are executive and professional in character. The local district system, still powerful in the South, needs likewise to be replaced by the county as the principal unit of support, organization and administration, and supervision. The proper and adequate education of the negro, one of the most confusing problems now facing the Southern states, is dealt with in Chapter XV.

The Southern states have always been primarily agricultural, and approximately 80 per cent of the people still live in rural sections, with farming as their occupation. The permanent prosperity and well-being of the South, therefore, depend upon the prosperity and well-being of the rural population. For this reason the strategic point in the South's future growth appears in the kind of provision that is made for the education of the rural people. Differences between the educational advantages provided for the children of the country and those provided for the children of the towns and cities are glaring. The rural school has not yet been standardized and modernized or touched by that spirit of improvement which has been marked in urban education, but the increasing interest in the consolidation of the small and ineffective schools into larger, better organized, better supported, and more closely supervised schools, is one of the hopeful signs of improvement. The building and maintenance of modern roads and highways, the encouragement of progressive methods of agriculture, the improvement of public health, are uniting with the movement for better rural schools to make rural life in the South more wholesome and inviting. Only by these means can real and lasting progress there be promoted. No material prosperity will be of advantage if the level of citizenship and public wholesomeness is not thereby advanced through education.

The material wealth of the South has grown great and apparent. The value of manufactured products is twice as great as that of the entire United States in 1880. During the last two decades the value of farm property has increased more than 400 per cent and the value of farm products nearly 600 per cent. The value of mineral products is six times as great as ten years ago. These facts not only reveal the industrial change but they furnish illustration of how intimately is the South related to the life of the whole country. The Southern states are no longer poor. In recent years they have made such a giant stride from poverty to prosperity that they are now able to do almost anything for public schools, public roads, and public health. The World War, moreover, not only revealed the weaknesses of education there, but it also helped the South to find herself. Under the impetus of the call to fight, to give, and to do for others what she had not felt fully able to do for herself, she found fresh hope and new energies. The call for food for our own and the soldiers of Europe, the campaign against waste, and the drives for the Red Cross and Liberty Bonds, led the South to thoughtful consideration of new enterprises and of old ones undeveloped. More nearly complete remedies for her shortcomings were thus revealed.

The measure of the South's conscience on schools and other means of intellectual progress must be taken neither from her impatience with unsympathetic and unintelligent criticism from without nor from her ability to build schools, but rather from her constantly growing need for education. Just as the chief problem of the South twenty-five years ago was to secure complete agreement on education, so to-day her chief need is *to educate*. The task to-day is little less conspicuous than then for its magnitude and difficulty. The task now is to build schools on a sound basis of financial support, professional direction, and supervision, so as to furnish every child equal educational rights — "the opportunity 'to burgeon out all that there is within him,'" to use the sentiment of the late Aycock, North Carolina's educational governor. Then, and then only, will the people of the South be enabled to observe fully, faithfully, and intelligently, their constantly enlarging relationships and, in the paraphrase of Jefferson, the earliest of the South's educational statesmen, to understand what goes on in the world and keep their part of it going right.

REFERENCES

COCHRAN, T. E. — *History of Education in Florida;* Lancaster, Pa., 1922.
Conference for Education in the South — *Proceedings.*
GARNER, JAMES W. (Editor) — *Studies in Southern History and Politics;* Columbia University Press, 1914.
General Education Board — *Public Education in North Carolina;* New York, 1921.
KNIGHT, EDGAR W.—*Public Education in the South;* Ginn, 1922.

KNIGHT, EDGAR W. — *Public School Education in North Carolina;* Houghton Mifflin, 1921.

Blue Book of Southern Progress; Manufacturers' Record Pub. Co. (Baltimore), 1922.

MURPHY, EDGAR G. — *Problems of the Present South;* Longmans Green, 1918.

NOBLE, STUART G. — *Forty Years of the Public Schools in Mississippi;* Teachers College, 1918.

PAGE, WALTER H. — *The Rebuilding of Old Commonwealths;* Doubleday, Page, 1905.

Peabody Board — *Proceedings of the Trustees.*

REISNER, EDWARD H. — *Nationalism and Education since 1789;* Macmillan, 1922.

United States Bureau of Education —
  Bulletin, 1912, No. 27, *History of Public Education in Arkansas.*
  Bulletin, 1915, No. 12, *History of Public Education in Alabama.*
  Bulletin, 1919, No. 14, *An Educational Study of Alabama.*
  Reports of the Commissioner of Education.

Virginia Public Schools — *Report of the Education Commission,* 1919.

www.ingramcontent.com/pod-product-compliance
Lightning Source LLC
Chambersburg PA
CBHW031715230426
43668CB00006B/226